AF469024

Yes! You Can Do Public Speaking

Yes! You Can Do Public Speaking

Tony Kenneson-Adams

A Gem from The Executive Solution

First published in England 2007

ISBN 978-1-84753-254-1

English edition 2007

To my wife, Aileen,
who taught me that to 'be' is enough.

Contents

Acknowledgements

There are so many people who have brought me to the place where I am able to write this book. So many of them helped me to believe I could be an effective public speaker.

To my Grandmother, who taught me I could be whatever I wanted to be. To all those who sat through my early efforts. To My wife Aileen whose patience allowed me to spend write this text. To Zoe, Nathan and Natalia, who taught me that I had to project my voice just to be heard.

Mostly, I would like to sincerely thank the people of Kosovo where so much of my public speaking and media work is grounded. The Kosovo people, who had suffered so much and had been left with so little, were always so warm and giving. It was a privilege to communicate with them and for them. Thanks to Arianeta, Tayota, Sasha, Armund, Fatos, Mimi and all the rest.

Finally, to those who have been so encouraging as a result of what they have learnt from this book and from my workshops.

To you all, thank you.

Tony Kenneson-Adams

Foreword

I recall that the first time I met Tony, I had only been talking to him for about five minutes when I first realised why I had come to the conclusion that he was special.

What started off as a bit of networking and general chit chat between two new friends seemed to very quickly turn into an audience with... I remember breaking away for a second to look behind me and noticed that a group of around ten people had joined our group to listen and wanting to speak with Tony.

I have rarely witnessed observing such an expert communicator in action. I began to ponder what was it that made somebody such a confident, engaging communicator, as I knew this was a life skill that pretty much all of my clients could benefit from.

I remember listening to Tony's stories with such interest. As each story unfolded, it cleverly uncovered many hidden metaphors and messages that allowed the listener to relate to Tony's experiences and each story gave the listener some new learning to take away. I was certain that this was a skill that could be taught, and I was fascinated to find out more.

I have memories of having to form a queue to wait to speak to Tony to ask him a question as he had become very popular in such a short space of time, largely because of his expert communication skills, but also because he is such a friendly and funny gentleman.

When my opportunity came to speak to him, I had only one question.

“Can you teach me to be as good a communicator in public as you are?”

“Yes, I can,” he replied simply.

Realising I had asked a pretty silly closed question, I followed it up with another. “Will you then?”

“Of course” he replied.

This was the beginning of a cascade of world class teaching that I realised very early on would be transferable to everyone. It does not matter what you do, I am guessing that there is a need for you to communicate in public at some stage of your day, whether that be at work in meetings and sales events, or even at home whilst socialising with friends.

I am absolutely delighted that Tony has agreed to write the second edition in the YES! YOU CAN series, and so generously share his profound knowledge, which he has gathered over a very lengthy period of time whilst lecturing, presenting and working for NATO, often addressing millions of people on live TV.

I am sure that you will find this book to be a very shrewd investment and an amazing read, but there is only one thing that beats theory and that’s getting out there and doing it.

I urge you to learn these great skills and techniques and then get out and try them on for size.

I wish you all the very best

David Knight CEO
www.TheExecutiveSolution.co.uk

YES YOU CAN DO PUBLIC SPEAKING

Part 1

> Put it before them briefly so they will read it, clearly so that they will appreciate it, picturesquely so they will remember it, and above all, accurately so they will be guided by its light.
>
> Joseph Pulitzer.

INTRODUCTION

Public speaking is not rocket science, but it does seem to fill people with either exhilaration or dread. In my experience as a former NATO spokesman and Lecturer, I have learnt to savour the personal and professional high that public speaking brings, a feeling that you can now experience by spending time reading and completing the exercises in this **Yes You Can** title. Being able to communicate and relay information that was saving lives on the streets of Pristina in the aftermath of the Kosovo war was a daily privilege and a pleasure, and **public speaking can now be a pleasure** for you too.

So why another book on public speaking? The majority of public speaking books are theoretical, others are by professional actors, still others by professional speakers and presenters. This book comes out of my experience from being firstly, an untrained amateur literally thrown into being a professional NATO spokesman, but more importantly, from what I learnt that will be of primary use to you either setting out in public speaking, or wishing to **improve on your skills**.

I was actually in my office in the UK one day as a Fast Jet Engineering Squadron Commander when the telephone rang and I was informed that I was going on immediate operations as the NATO Command Spokesman to Kosovo. I was not a professional TV speaker or Press Relations Officer, but I quickly had to become one. Because of the imperative to get to Kosovo, there was no time for training, and within twenty-four hours of arriving in Pristina Kosovo, I was giving my first live TV interview.

Therefore, this book tracks what I learned on the job. What worked and what didn't work, and more importantly, what I wish I had known and practised before I got on the plane heading for what had been Yugoslavia.

I have used these practical lessons to train others in public speaking, including those who have English as a second language. These methods work and I encourage you to follow the exercises to **build your confidence** and become a competent public speaker.

The Pen is Mightier than the Sword

The pen is mightier than the sword, and the spoken word can be mightier still. '**Yes! You Can Be An Efficient Public Speaker**' will give you the same skills and confidence that I have gained as a lecturer, professional speaker, trainer and TV spokesman.

However, this book is not just only for the professional press spokesman, teacher, manager or executive; it is written in accessible **language for you**. Through simple methodologies and exercises, you will learn how anyone, including you, can become an accomplished public speaker.

Phobia or Opportunity

On any list of phobias in English-speaking countries, public speaking is always in the top two along with fear of spiders. Yet 99.9% of us are engaged in public speaking everyday, at work, in the shops or at the bus queue. So what is it about the formalised act of speaking to groups of people that strikes fear into the hearts of rational individuals? Principally, I believe it is the fear of failure, of messing up; it's the fear of being embarrassed.

But this fear is irrational and is based in physiology and not in our ability, especially once we are trained.

Physiology not Fact.

Don't be Hostage to the Cave Man.

Way back in our evolutionary past, we developed the hormone adrenaline. This hormone was excreted into the bloodstream when our ancestors found themselves in new or difficult circumstances. It gave heightened senses and the ability to react quickly, to run away, or to stand and fight. Useful if you were faced by a sabre-toothed tiger, but not useful in today's world. Thus, if you are nervous about the situation of public speaking, your physiology is saying, "do you want to fight or run away?" So as you get the knot in your stomach, your mouth dries up, and your palms get sweaty, it is a response to an ancient situation. It is not relevant today. But in recognising this, we can use it. We can allow the adrenaline to heighten our awareness of the situation, to make us alive to the possibilities of heightening our performance. Thus, wait for that adrenaline rush, acknowledge it and use it.

Success Breeds Success

If you have a fear of public speaking, you should first bring to remembrance other occasions when you have had to complete a task that you were nervous about, and yet you completed it successfully. Perhaps giving blood, taking an exam, going for an interview. Now remember the feeling when you succeeded. Bring that success back to your memory and really think about it. What did it feel like, imagine it as a picture on a TV screen. What colours can you see, how does it sound. What does your picture of **success feel** like? Now make the colours and the feelings more intense, amplify that feeling of success, brighten those colours and turn up the sound of success. Now expand the picture bigger and bigger, until the picture is the size of a cinema screen. Feel the confidence that your previous now-amplified success brings. **Feel the excitement of success**. Hold and continue to amplify that thought throughout your journey to become an effective public speaker.

Now transfer that energy to thinking about public speaking, bringing in your success. You see, if you can feel your success before the event, then you can enjoy your success before you even begin the talk. So often, people say, "I have a sense of impending doom about public speaking." Or, "I just know something is going to go wrong." What you must do is to flip that negative attitude of something is going to go wrong, to a confident positive that, "**I have a feeling of impending success**". It is only habit and culture those makes us expect to fail. This book will teach you to expect success as a habit in your public speaking.

Preparation Amplifies Success

To build for your success, the correct preparation is essential. With the correct preparation you can be confident that **you will not mess up** and thus fear of messing up is not relevant.

Public speaking is, in its simplest form, merely speaking in public. No great revelation there. We do it every day, at home, in work and in public situations. We speak in public all the time. Think now why some times your 'public speaking' has been more effective than at other times. One of the main reasons will be preparation. With proper preparation we have pre-knowledge of what we expect of ourselves, we have the facts, we have thought through what we need to say, and we deliver the message confidently. This same process will stand you in good stead whether you are telephoning a plumber, giving a wedding speech, giving a sales presentation or being interviewed by the BBC.

Remember the five Ps!

Prior

Preparation

Prevents

Poor

Performance

Try the following exercise.

Let's see where you are currently. Using the format below, write down a series of memories of a particular piece of public speaking or conversation. Write down one thing that went well about it and one thing that went badly.

Event	Addressed the PTA
Good element	Explained what needed to be done to improve school security.
Bad element	Tried to open with a joke but it was a disaster.
Lesson learned	Humour is not my forte.

Event	Went to see the bank manager for a loan.
Good element	I was on time.
Bad element	Completely forgot all of the good reasons why he should give me the loan.
Lesson learned	Write out a script.

Now write out a few of your own examples.

Event --

Good element --

Bad element --

Lesson learned --

Event --

Good element --

Bad element --

Lessons learned --

Event --

Good element --

Bad element --

Lessons learned --

Event --

Good element --

Bad element --

Lessons learned --

So, let us review your past work and what you have learnt about your performance. Note the good and bad points. It is good to remember the bad points, as these are what you should work on, or perhaps avoid altogether. The good points show you that you are already doing better than you thought, and these will be the basis on which you can practice and improve your public speaking skill.

Establishing Rapport.

The next element that is essential for successful public speaking after preparation is to establish rapport. Rapport gets your audience on side and in the correct frame of mind to listen to what you have to say. Rapport is established in the following ways:

- Being authentic and honest.
- Establishing eye contact.
- Dressing appropriately.
- Hitting the right level.
- Knowing your audience.
- Charisma.

Authentic and Honest

Your demeanour, body language, and verbal language are received and interpreted by your audience on two levels: the conscious and the subconscious. If you arrive dressed as a clown for a boardroom presentation, your audience would understandably disregard you. But the human subconscious is just as quick to notice if you are wearing a metaphoric 'red nose.' You will not be able to fool an audience for long, so just don't try.

Fake it and be Found Out

I remember attending one briefing where a very senior Turkish representative gave a presentation to the senior officers and representatives of the NATO countries. The Turkish representative read his presentation word for word. At the end of his presentation, and without asking for questions, the presenter moved to sit down. One of the delegates stopped the official in his tracks and asked him a simple question. From the presenter's reaction, it was obvious that the official not only could not answer the question, but neither could he understand English. He had been coached for the one presentation. It was obvious to everyone, even without the question from the journalist, that not only was he 'wearing the red nose', but the rotating tie and big boots as well.

Establishing Eye Contact

This does not mean staring everybody down, but it does mean working the room. You should ensure that you are constantly changing your gaze and regularly making contact with as many people as possible. This brings them into your zone and makes what you are saying personal to them. This works well with an audience up to about 100. After that, you can't look directly into everyone's eyes. In this case, you should mentally divide the audience into sections and make eye contact with the sections in the same way that you would do with individuals. This will enable you to see if your audience is staying with you. Are they interested, are they confused, are they bored? Are you pitching your presentation at the right level? Read their faces. Once you can read your audience with eye contact, you will maintain rapport and then you will find it is easier to speak and to lead your audience on the journey of education and information.

Dressing Appropriately

This may sound obvious, but believe me I have seen many people, including professional presenters, dressed inappropriately. The guides I would use are:

1. Dress in the style of your audience; if you are not sure what the dress of the day will be, ask the organiser.

2. For formal presentations, wear formal clothes that will convey an air of authority.

3. If you are wearing a long sleeve shirt, wear a tie. The total image is important.

4. For informal occasions such as the company picnic, still make sure you look good so as not to detract from what you are saying.

5. Don't wear outrageous patterns or colours; they will detract from what you have to say. An audience will need little reason to spend their time considering your poor dress sense and not listen to your words.

<u>Exercise</u>

Try going through your wardrobe combining your outfits whilst standing in front of a mirror. What do you think looks good for different types of presentation? Now show your partner, friend or co-worker and ask what they think looks good. You may be in for some surprises. Remember, you are looking to add to your overall presentation, not detract from it so don't be precious. Are you wearing the correct colours for your complexion, age body shape, etc? A great piece of advice is to contact a style coach or colourist. One session will make an enormous difference to add to your presentation. If you don't want to employ a style coach, buy one of the various 'what not to wear books.' Do yourself a favour, use how you look to empower your words and not detract from them. More tips on this later.

Hitting the Right Level

Before you sit down to plan what you will say or how you will say it, you must know whom you are presenting to. What level should you aim at? Teenagers need a different approach than adults. Sales staff will need a different approach and language than senior executives. The content of your message could be almost the same, but you will need to match your language, pace, and level to your audience. You should also ask how big is the hall and how many will be in your audience?

Charisma

Charisma is the Holy Grail of public speaking. Charisma itself means 'god given'. Now if you have the 'god given' charisma of Martin Luther King, or the inspiration of JFK or Winston Churchill, you are 80% of the way to perfectly delivered public speaking. But if you are one of the vast majority who at least do not **feel charismatic**, there is still plenty of hope. Firstly, many individuals can 'act' charisma for the period of their public speaking. You will all have seen massively charismatic actors in films, but when they are being interviewed as themselves, they could not be more boring or un-inspirational or un-charismatic. However, you can fake charisma.

Mirroring

Charles Bronson once said, "The only thing that you cannot fake is sincerity, and when you have learnt to fake that, then you can do anything." In essence actors, but also business people and especially politicians, as well as the 'cult of celebrity' have often just learnt to fake sincerity, charisma, inspiration and many other characteristics that most of us believe cannot be faked. Thus, you too can act or just fake charisma by practice. Copy how actors or TV personalities look and speak when they are being charismatic. Is it a look, a stance, their voice, their clothes, do they lower the pitch of their voice, is it how they stand, is it vocabulary or appearing to be a little aloof? Try copying what you admire in other people to find your own charismatic presenting persona. This is known as mirroring and is a technique on which Negro-Linguistic Programming was founded, which is now used by professional coaches to enable their usually ordinary clients to learn to do extraordinary things.

Coaching

Your journey or your goal in improving anything, including your effectiveness in public speaking is 'Getting from a present state to a desired state'. Always have a goal in mind when you are working on an issue that you want to improve. A 1000 mile journey may begin with one step, but you have to know where you are going before you put your shoes on. How else will you know when you have arrived? Therefore continually measure your progress honestly and record your thoughts. This will provide constant encouragement to you when those niggling doubts rear their ugly heads.

Planning Your Presentation is Just ABCD

The primary method that I teach that will facilitate your development success is simply based on the letters **ABCD**. This method is particularly useful if you have little or no time to organise your thoughts; it is also an excellent skeleton on which to 'hang' your presentation if you have time to plan your talk. This is because this method is simplicity itself, as all you have to remember is **ABCD**. Whilst in Kosovo I was often called to incidents or contacted by the press moments after an event and before I had the facts. This **ABCD** method enabled me to quickly prepare a presentation to give the media what they needed, giving myself only a few minutes to obtain and to consider reactions to the bare facts. Once you get this method established in your mind, the method will organise the key to a successful presentation for you.

I am of the firm conviction that anyone can be an effective public speaker by observing my simple **A, B, C, D** formula.

A = Accuracy.
B = Brevity.
C = Clarity.
D = Delivery.

Accuracy

One of the essentials of public speaking is the accuracy of the information that you are delivering. If you stand in front of people, they are immediately putting you in a place of authority. For your authority to last for more than just one presentation, it must be credible. Essential to credibility is truth. Everything that you put over must be accurate on each and every occasion. Check your facts at least twice. You cannot regain credibility without the passage of considerable time, if at all, and time is a commodity that you rarely have with the press especially. You should never try and bluff information as someone will always find you out and it is you who will lose your credibility. With the ease of use of search engines, there is no excuse for wrong or inaccurate information.

Brevity

> **'I am sorry this letter is so long, I haven't had the time to write a shorter one."**
>
> **Winston Churchill**

Brevity is a skill to be practised, as you need to condense your message to the essential detail, however complex that may be. Try this exercise:

Exercise

Your objective in this exercise is to reduce this passage from 240 words to 120 words or less whilst retaining the thread of the story.

Lieutenant Colonel Simon O'Brian was on his first foot patrol in Pristina Kosovo in the former Yugoslavia. This was the first time for some while that he had proceeded on an operation without his regiment, who were still on rotation at Alexandra Barracks in Belfast, Northern Ireland. Simon had spent 25 years in the army, all of which had been spent as an Officer in the 'Duke of 'Boots' and much of it as a specialist Bomb Disposal Officer (BDO). Simon was coming up to the end of his service in the Army and had only 18 months before he retired at the young age of 44. Kosovo would be his last operational tour, and strangely it was not as a BDO, but as the NATO Spokesman for the three star General who was the commander for the Kosovo Force. Simon had had only a week's leave with Rose, his wife, and his two children before leaving for Kosovo, and he had left his home in Salisbury after another blazing argument. Simon had found out that Rose was in the throes of another affair, but this time she had been highly indiscreet and everyone in the Regiment knew that she was sleeping with a junior NCO, a Corporal that, in fact, worked for Simon. Simon was only too happy to be out of the marital strife, and though he missed his kids, the back streets of Pristina seemed strangely welcoming.

Clarity

Clarity of your message is essential; you cannot leave yourself open to more than the interpretation that you intended for your message. It is not your audience's fault if they take a different meaning from your presentation than that which you intended. You must ensure your message is completely clear. Use of metaphors, for example, can be particularly dangerous, especially if using an interpreter. An example that springs to mind, that caused me some embarrassment when I was speaking in Serbia through an interpreter.

It's a Pipe Dream, or is it!

In explaining that nowhere was ever completely without crime, I stated that, "100% security was a pipe dream." Which seemed clear to me. For example, there are victims of gun crime everywhere from Manchester to Chicago, from Deli to Sydney. However, the expression 'pipe dream' does not exist in Serbian. So the translation went into the media as, "100% security is an old man sitting on a porch smoking a pipe." This was clearly not my intention. My advice is, "Say what you mean and mean what you say."

Delivery

So much of what you want to say can be negated by a poor delivery. Just thinking about these issues will incrementally improve your delivery. However, the single most important tool to improve your delivery is practice. This is where you need to stand in front of a full-length mirror or use a video recorder, to get an audience perspective of what you look like and sound like. If you are doing something that annoys you, it will annoy your audience. An audience is so easily distracted and will happily concentrate on how many times you say, "um" or "as you know" or "ah" or cough, or jingle your keys, rather than listen to your message. Try it yourself, watch someone else present and count how many times they say "um" and then, when they have finished, try and recall what they said.

Position

If you are standing, stand with your feet in a T position. This will stop you rocking backwards and forwards and rising up on your toes, believe me it happens. Clear your pockets of keys and coins and then if you 'talk with your hands,' keep them in your pockets. Learn which mannerisms are annoying and coach yourself out of them. 'Um', 'er', scratching, sniffing, whatever it is you see on video playback or when in front of that mirror. If you are sitting, sit up straight, and make sure you pull your shirt, jacket or dress down at the back and sit on it, so as to ensure you don't look like you have grown a hump on your back.

Exercise

Try this exercise. Deliver a five-minute talk to yourself about your life to this point. Watch out for your mannerisms and make a conscious effort to coach them out. Content is irrelevant for this exercise.

How did that go? Let's look in more detail at some of the things that may have happened.

Run out of steam.

It is amazing that on a subject of which you are the only expert, you run out of things to say. At this stage that is unimportant, as the rest of this book will show you how to construct content and talks to time. The important thing at this point is that you get an initial understanding that time can seem to stretch or constrict when you are speaking.

Feeling Self Conscious

This is completely normal, and it will keep you humble. Re-run the exercise and see how it feels a second time and a third time. Now how does it feel, better? Not to worry, it will.

Mannerisms

How many mannerisms did you find, two, five, ten? Not to worry. Note them down below and be conscious of them, each one you identify becomes a strength as you can coach yourself out of it.

MY MANNERISMS

1.

2.

3.

4.

5.

6.

7.

8.

9.

10.

Accent and Dialect

Accent and dialect are fine if your audience can understand them. But remember your main objective is to communicate and so you may have to sacrifice a little individuality for clarity. Again, a voice coach is an excellent help in this, or alternately you can try this exercise.

Exercise

Get hold of a broad sheet newspaper and begin to read the articles aloud in the accent of a BBC Newsreader; a typical home counties neutral accent. As you listen carefully to your own voice, be conscious to remove the modulations of your voice that come from your regional accent.

Exercise

Whilst in your car or whilst lying in the bath, recite a nursery rhyme or poem over and over while hearing that same Home Counties 'neutral' accent in your head. Soften the vowels and consonants. Then return to your natural accent and compare how they sound. Learn to transit between the two to maximise the impact of clarity on your potential audience. You can also try reciting the passage below in front of the mirror trying the neutral and your natural accent.

Of all the Snodgobblers that lived on the banks of the Uske river, Emis was above all the strangest but yet the most special. His fiery red hair stuck out awkwardly like tangled straw and his tiny fat legs grew out of an over- plump body. His skinny arms seemed to belong to someone else and his three long fingers looked like curled autumn leaves. His ruddy red face was etched with a permanent smile, and his pointy blue ears, that shone in the dark, had such acute hearing he could hear a mouse scratching its nose in the nettles at the bottom of the garden. Such was a Snodgobbler in its natural form, but more of that later.

Using Your Voice

Think back to some famous speeches from great orators. They are easy to find on the internet. Listen to the colour in the speaker's voice. What makes the speaker voice special that you can model?

Vocabulary

There are many elements in the use of vocabulary that can be used to enhance your speech, such as the way you can use the variety and beauty of the words of the English language. There is a rich diversity of words that can be 'played' with in English to say the same thing, look at the word 'excellence' for example. You could use goodness, quality, worth, richness, value, etc, etc. Do not restrict your language; vary your vocabulary and have a thesaurus by your side as you put your script together.

Modulation

A monotone voice will send an audience to sleep in minutes. Modulation is how you raise and lower the pitch of your voice; you do it in normal conversation every day. Listen to speakers on the TV and radio news, and again model how they use their voices.

Emphasis

Where you place the emphasis in a sentence will drastically alter the meaning of the sentence. Read out the following sentences, emphasising the highlighted word and note how the meaning of sentence changes as you emphasise each word in turn. This is a good skill to master for your own presentations.

I did not say she stole the money.

I **did** not say she stole the money.

I did **not** say she stole the money.

I did not **say** she stole the money.

I did not say **she** stole the money.

I did not say she **stole** the money.

I did not say she stole **the** money.

I did not say she stole the **money**.

Pace

If modulation is the vertical change in the pitch of your voice, then pace is the horizontal change. Again, in normal conversation you speed up and slow down your voice without thinking about it. This variety brings colour and interest to your voice. Your voice is an amazing instrument that can be used to enhance what you say to take your audience on an amazing journey. Think of the differences of voice used by personalities, actors, and comedians. Study how Matt Lucas uses his voice in his Little Britain characters. Fast high pitch will bring excitement and enthusiasm, but danger of annoyance if you stay there too long. Low pitch, slow pace will bring thoughtfulness, but danger of sleep if you stay without variance. Master this and you will be able to roam around the range of your voice to exploit its qualities.

Try saying the following in all areas of modulation and pace of your voice and note how the mood changes.

Vicky the Vampire Vaulted the Van; Billy the Bulldog Borrowed a Bone.

SPEED

FAST/HIGH	FAST/LOW
SLOW/FAST	SLOW/LOW

RANGE

You should aim for your voice to move around it range of pitch, pace and modulation to make your presentation engaging.

Pauses

> The notes I handle no better than many other pianists. But the pauses between the notes – ah, that is where the art resides.
> Arthur Schnabel

Pauses add power and panache to your presentations. Pauses can be used to emphasise a point or stop to make the audiences think. They can also be used for you to think about your next thought or point or to check that you are maintaining rapport.

Projection

There is little point going through all the effort in preparing for a session of public speaking if nobody can hear you. However, projection is about more than just volume, projection is not shouting. The easiest way I believe you can visualise projection is by imagining that you are forcing your voice up the side of a rainbow, and watching it land in the ears of the person furthest away at the bottom of the other side of the rainbow. To do this, you must stand up straight, shoulders back, speak moderately slowly, confidently and with just sufficient volume. If you are not using any form of amplification, then ask if they can hear you at the back or practice with someone else in the room before your audience arrives. However, be aware that sound will soon be attenuated when the room is full of bodies. That means you will need to speak up just a little more when your audience arrives.

Plan for Success

What the thinker thinks, the prover proves.

Every single time you get up to speak, you must do it with the complete knowledge that you will be a tremendous success. You start this by visualising your success based on the fact that you have done your research, you have prepared what you want to say and you are going to establish rapport with your audience. You are going to be interesting and you have something people want to hear. You have put in the effort and you will be a success. You should start enjoying that success before you get up to speak, because if you are enjoying your success before you start speaking, you have already given yourself the mental advantage.

Distractions

In public speaking, it is important to be known for your reactions even more than your actions.

We live in a noisy world. As soon as you start speaking, you will begin to notice how noisy it is. Cars, children, aircraft, sweet papers, chairs scraping on the floor, champagne corks, coughing, heckling, drunks and the modern pain: the mobile phone. If you are new to public speaking, the best thing is to try and ignore it. Depending on circumstances, you can ask for the person introducing you to request that everyone turns off their mobile phones, but you can guarantee that there will be someone in the audience who thinks they are far too important to turn theirs off.

I trust that you will not have a distraction that I experienced when giving a live TV interview in Kosovo. I had just made my initial statement about Kosovo now being a ‘safe and secure’ area with 95% security across the province and was opening up for questions, when the unmistakable sound of an AK-47 semi-automatic rifle cracked across the UN compound.

The correct thing to do would have been to ‘duck and cover,’ but I was on TV, and being British, and as the single burst was not followed up by anything else and nobody was hurt, I shrugged my shoulders and said straight to the camera, “Almost 95% security has been achieved.” What can you do?

If you are distracted, don't get flustered. Take a deep breath, pause, check your notes if you need to and then continue. Remember that the 'show must go on.' If you react as though you are unfazed, two things will happen. Firstly, your confidence will improve, and secondly your audience will have noticed the noise, sympathised with you and will admire your skill in recovery, thus increasing rapport and listening to you even more intently. Use everything as an opportunity to increase your confidence and credibility.

Speaking for Yourself or As a Spokesperson

Speaking as a Spokesperson for somebody else or for an organisation, is just an extension of public speaking. Ideally you will receive some specific company training, but never fear this section will give you what you need to stand out as an excellent spokesperson. But beware, this is an area in which you have to be very careful.

If you are speaking in your own right, you are answerable only to yourself. If you are speaking on behalf of an organisation, then your opinions are irrelevant. In fact, you may have to adopt the organisation's vocabulary and even a point of view with which you may not agree. That is irrelevant. When you are being paid to be the public face of the organisation, you are giving the organisation's message and not your own. You will have a standard set of answers to possible questions that you will be continually working up, trying to imagine what questions you would ask in a particular situation, and recording the answers on paper from the company point of view for future use. Irrespective of how difficult a question may be:

- You should never lie, as your credibility will be blown instantly.
- If you do not know the answer, say so, and tell the inquirer that you will get back to them.
- Never waffle.
- ABCD.

If you are being pressured to give an answer that you need company advice on and you are not prepared to answer, tell the inquirer so. If they are presenting you with a fact that you need further advice on use, "I cannot confirm or deny" and pass on the answer when it has been cleared by the company or organisation. Above all maintain control of you integrity and the situation. This can be difficult and so here is an example.

I was once giving a major press conference at which I was announcing that we had captured three terrorist suspects on behalf of the International Court in the Hague. They would soon be extradited for trial. This was a major news story. Somehow, one of the journalists had some information that should not have been in the public domain.

"Why is it that the fourth suspect got away, doesn't this make your mission a failure and not a success." Stated the journalist

At that stage, I knew that we had not apprehended the fourth subject, but that we did know where he was and that we would be taking further action later. However, I was not authorised to issue any detail on the forth suspect. How would you have dealt with this situation?

____

____

____

____

____

____

My answer was, "We are here today to announce that a successful operation was carried out this morning and that three terrorist suspects have been apprehended and will be heading for trial. I can neither confirm nor deny any other detail." I then had to check back with my superiors for their instructions. They wanted a complete blackout on any other details for 24 hours, at which time we had the fourth suspect in custody. This is obviously an extreme example, but it will hold you in good stead for any situation that you may come across. The other thing that you should find out is if your organisation has already decided upon a 'holding answer' for an expected question. The companies legal department will have cleared this and thus you should not detract from it at all.

Sound Bites

When speaking for TV or radio, you must remember that the media are looking for a sound bite that they will use for their reports. A 15, 30 or even 60-minute interview will often be reduced to a 9-second sound bite. In exceptional circumstances, with a major story that is complex and needs more explanation, you may get 30 seconds, but that is major coverage for a TV or radio channel. Therefore, to ensure that they get the 9 seconds that you want aired, make it clear which 9 seconds that you want them to carry.

You can do this by ensuring that you give them the sound bite that sums up the story. State your sound bite at the beginning of your presentation and repeat it at the end, and also slip it in the middle of your interview if it is appropriate. Journalists love others to do their work for them so you can use this to your advantage. Be aware of what they want and give it to them on a plate. Also, remember that all answers must lead back to your message. You can promote this by giving your prepared answers to whatever the question is that they may ask. A good phrase to use to manipulate this is:

"That is a good question, but the real question that you should be asking is ......" and give a stock answer or an answer to a point that you want to emphasise.

Pre-Interview Preparation

Before the interview and as far in advance as possible, you should agree upon some ground rules with the journalist.

1. Is this a background interview? If this is the case, you must make it clear that everything that is discussed is off the record and not for publication. Journalists often need background, especially on complex issues. I have never had journalists attribute background information having previously set the ground rules.

2. Discuss the scope of the interview so that you can adequately research the topic and get clearance if you require it.

3. Ask what the first question will be so that you can flow straight into the interview to settle yourself down. However, do not become overconfident as it can floor you if the question takes an unexpected twist.

I was once given 48 hours notice to prepare for an interview, which would be on the record. In was also to be on a live TV link to Sweden on Health and Safety risks for soldiers operating in Kosovo. I was expecting to speak about the hazards of air pollution, water pollution, unexploded ordnance, etc. We agreed that the first question would be a general question about Health and Safety issues for the soldiers. What actually was asked was "What are the Health and Safety issues for foreign soldiers that use local prostitutes?" This was certainly off message, and not what I had prepared for.

My answer was, "I have no knowledge of such issues, the interesting question you should be asking is….." I was being careful not to use the journalist's words, in case it was aired/cut. I have to say this was after I had gained considerable experience. If I had not been completely sure of my facts and myself, I would have said, "That question is outside of the scope of this interview. I will be happy to discuss such issues in a future interview." I have to add that this is the only time such a thing has happened, and may have been due to me working with this particular journalist for the first time. The acid test is to 'Stay on message unless you are accomplished and confident.'

Beginning, Middle, End

A good speech is like a good story, it needs a beginning middle and end. The beginning has to grip the audience and reel them in, the end has to summarise and ensure that they have something to take away with them. The middle develops your point and takes your audience on a journey. It is essential that the beginning of your speech be so gripping that the audience is drawn into your story and want to listen for more.

A useful opener is to start with a statistic, a famous quote, or a controversial sentence, if you can use it and if it is appropriate, you could use humour. You should also establish your credibility as soon as possible so your audience knows that you are speaking as an authority on your subject.

I particularly like to use quotes or statistics. These are readily available in purpose-written books and on Internet sites. If you are going to use quotes, make sure they will be from someone who they know, or say something with which your audience can associate. They must also be attributed to the originator.

A few examples.

"Parenthood is part joy, part guerrilla warfare."

Ed Asner, International Parent Coach

"I had to do everything that Fred had to do, but backwards and in high heels."

Ginger Rogers

"Plan your routine and routinely plan."

Tony Kenneson-Adams

Also, don't be afraid to quote yourself, as above, or even make something up, for example;

" As a famous explorer once said, when there is a lion in your tent, you don't worry about the colour of your socks."

It's your presentation; **you're in charge.** There is an annex of quotes at the end of this book to help you start your presentations.

<u>Exercise</u>

You are the head of the Criminal Investigation Bureau. It is the evening shift and you have to write a briefing for a 'sting' to be carried out at midnight. The briefing that must last exactly five minutes is based around the story of Little Red Riding Hood with a modern update. Your task is to put together the five-minute briefing. First, write five points for each section of your brief. Just take the facts from memory. This will form the skeleton of your briefing.

Beginning

1---

2---

3---

4---

5---

Middle

1---

2---

3---

4---

5---

<u>End</u>

1---

2---

3---

4---

5---

For the beginning section, you may have something like:

Beginning

1. Crime figures have risen by 45% in just three weeks.
2. Little Red AKA 'The Hood' is suspected to be active in the area after a period of absence.
3. Little Red has been seen acting suspiciously. We expect that she is preparing to 'make a drop.'
4. The location of the drop is expected to be at the headquarters of a local Mafia Boss, AKA 'The God Mother.'
5. All units should be ready to move at five minutes to midnight.

When you have the three sets of five points, link them together firstly in sections, and then as a complete story.

When you have completed the whole story, read it out loud. How does it sound? Does the beginning hold your attention? Does the story develop in a convincing way? Does the end summarise what you have had to say and leave the listener with some sort of a lesson? Is it exactly five minutes long? If it is not keep adjusting the story until it is?

You should carry on with updating this exercise until the presentation is in a position where you think it is ready for delivery. Whenever possible, I write set pieces ahead of time and then leave it for a day or two. I then go back to it and update and fine-tune it.

Other Presentation Preparation Methods

Lotus Method

The lotus method is another way not only to organise your data, but also to extract facts and direct your research. Let us say that you are preparing a talk titled, "Shark –The Fascinating Fish."

Step 1 – Prepare a three by three grid.
Step 2 – Place your subject in the centre.
Step 3 – In the surrounding eight squares, begin to develop your presentation, one new point per square.
Step 4 – For each of the eight points, create another grid, etc.

Perfectly camouflaged	Perfect killing machine	Evolutionary Marvel
Found in over 2/3 of the world's oceans	**SHARK – the fascinating fish**	Same design for over one million years
Most weird eye adaptation – Hammer Head	Most misunderstood fish – Great White	Largest fish in the ocean –Whale shark*

Sometimes feeds vertically	Little known about migration habits.	Over 13 ½ tones.
Egg case is two feet long	**Whale Shark***	Largest 60 feet long
Many killed by boating accidents	Brings in tourists	Only eats plankton

By the time you have completed this exercise, which you can do with a friend or a group, you will have enough information for several talks.
I once used this method for a talk on the differences in shark's teeth. This method once gave me enough detail to fill a 40-minute presentation.

Mind Map

The mind map is used to elicit and organise information that can then be used to prepare your presentation. Let's look at a mind map for a talk on mountaineering.

In this method, you simply place your topic in the middle of the page and develop layers of thinking that move to the edge of the paper. Use as big a sheet of paper as you can. Remember that your talk needs a beginning, middle and end. Alternately, an introduction, development and conclusion.

This develops naturally as your thought process in the mind map develops.

PLANNING A MOUNTAINEERING EXPEDITION

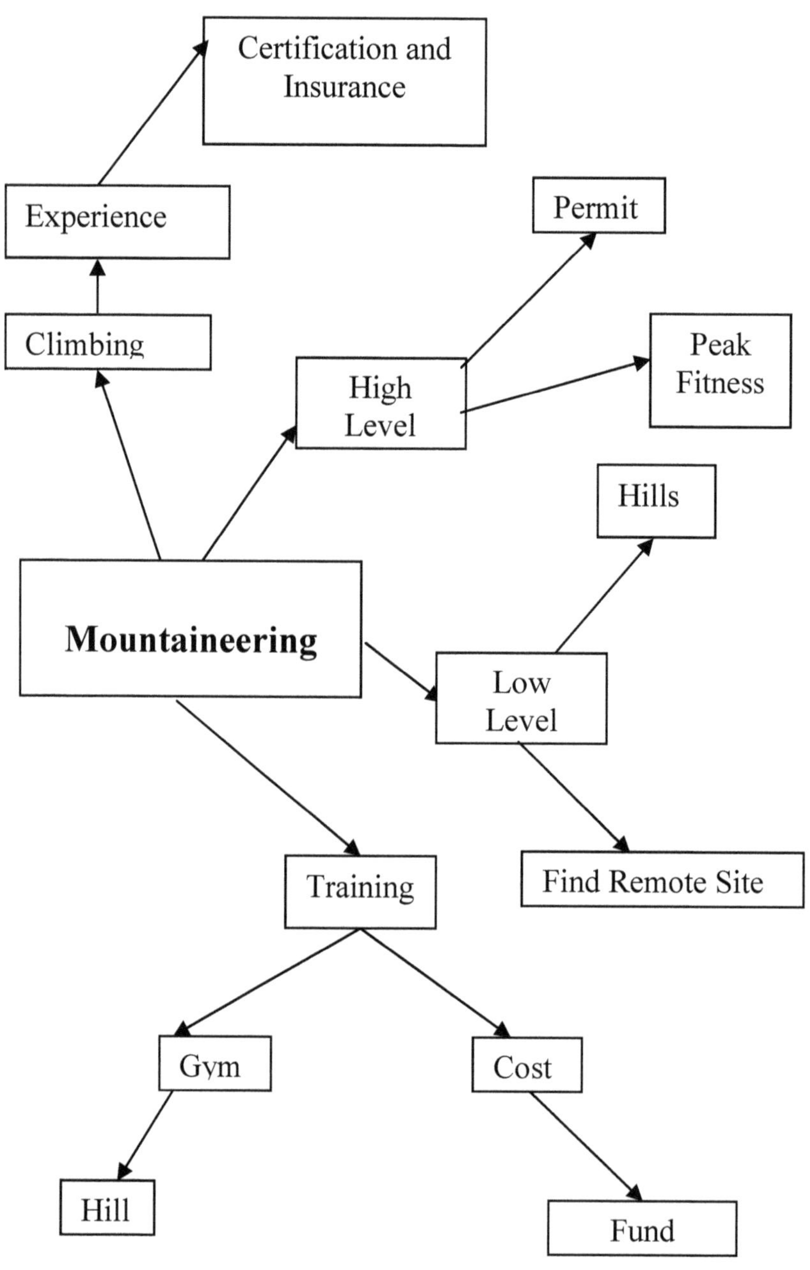

Other Preparations for Public Speaking

As well as knowing what to say and how to say it, what else do you need to know? Consider the following points:

Who are you talking to?

Do you understand your audience?

How many people are you talking to, and will you be using amplification?

Can you get some experience with the room or amplification ahead of time?

Where are you speaking?

Plan a route to get to the location ahead of time.

You should be at least a half an hour early to meet with your contact if necessary.

Have a look at the room or location that you are speaking in. If you are using visual aids, make sure that you plan all the equipment that you will need. Do you need to bring a laptop and projector, or can you just take a USB stick or CD? Leave nothing to chance. You should also be able to deliver your presentation without electronic media, as technology could always let you down when you most need it.

By writing out and re-reading your talk you should have the flow of your talk and the main points all committed to memory. You can always have the whole speech on paper or in key points in front of you if you have developed it as I have suggested above. You can also just use your key points as the milestones for your talk. However, resist the temptation to just read out your script for all the reasons already discussed. Remember rapport is established and maintained by personality and eye contact. There will be little personality and zero eye contact if you revert to just reading your script.

It is also important to be aware that the unexpected and the unplanned seem to become like a moth to flame when you are a public speaker. So be flexible and do not loose your cool when things conspire against you.

For example:

The San Marco Brief.

I had prepared for a briefing to the press corps for a major NATO exercise. The plan was that the General would arrive and give a five-minute introduction, followed by my briefing, followed by the General taking questions. The General was flying in by helicopter. I had arrived early and checked the location, power, laptop, projector, screen and I had my presentation slides on a CD and in hardcopy to hand to the journalists. The presentation was planned to take place in a large tent.

Five minutes before the presentation, the General radioed ahead to say that he would do a low-level fly-past and start the exercise from the air. He would land at 5pm for questions. However, the press needed 'copy' at 4pm to meet the evening deadline, and they wanted to be outside for the start of the exercise that started with a parachute drop.

Bugger!!!

The plan had to change, the presentation was scrapped and I briefed the press 'on-the-hoof' on the field of operations, using my notes. I then held the press conference and the journalists went off to their editors with copy. The lesson that I learned is flexibility is the key. Be prepared to change your plan at any time. Remember flexibility is an attitude of mind that is enabled by thorough preparation.

Asking Questions?

When you are making the presentation, you set the rules for questions. Many circumstances for public speaking do not call for questions, for example, the best man's speech. However, if you are making a presentation at work or to the media, you should be prepared for questions, and thus you set the agenda.

Firstly, you should state whether you wish to take questions as you proceed through your presentation or whether you will take questions at the end. I always take questions at the end of my presentation rather than during it for the following reasons:

- You can easily lose your chain of thought.
- Your talk to become disjointed.
- It to become difficult to develop your argument.
- When the journalist is talking, you are not.
- It is more difficult for TV and Radio editors to put your words together in a meaningful way for TV or radio.

Remember that you can use questions to your advantage to re-emphasise your point, so don't shy away from them.
For example:

Question: How many bombs were dropped in the Kosovo war?

Answer: That is a good question, but more importantly, what was the effect on the people that were liberated as a result of that bombing.

In this example:

1. I didn't know the exact number of bombs so I didn't attempt an answer.
2. I turned the question to my positive press line.
3. I used it as a bridge to start talking about repatriation of refugees.

Use every opportunity to guide questioning to your advantage.

Always remember that you can decide not to answer a question or you can arrange the answer for a later date. Don't speculate, don't try and wing it. Do remember Accuracy, Brevity, Clarity, and Delivery.

Types of Questions

You should expect two types of questions: open questions and closed questions. Closed questions are answered with a simple yes or no, and unless you wish to use the question to your advantage, leave it at that. Do not be tempted to compensate for a poor question by giving away unnecessary information, unless you are doing it to your own advantage. Closed questions are not good technique, as they do not give information, they only check facts.

Good questions are open questions that make the presenter think and answer in sentences. Good questions usually start with:

Who.
What.
When.
How.
Why.
Tell me.

Here is an example of how the same question can be asked at three different levels to gather more and more information.

Level 1

Q1. Do you have any children?

A1. Yes.

Level 2

Q2. How many children do you have at school?

A2. I have a daughter and a son at school and an older daughter at university.

Level 3

Q3. Tell me about your children?

A3. I have three children, two girls and a boy. Two of them are twins, a boy and a girl aged 16 and they are at college. My son is training to be a carpenter and my daughter wants to be an accountant. My eldest daughter is at university studying graphic arts and is doing very well. Their hobbies are .... etc.

By understanding questions, you will be better prepared for the answers. Try this exercise.

Exercise

Develop the questions below to the three levels, to illicit deeper and more detailed information, and explore this questioning technique.

1. Do you have a job?

2. ....

3. ....

1. What is your hobby?

2. ....

3 ....

1. Where do you live?

2. ....

3. ....

Acting Methodology For Professional Presenting

There are many lessons that public speakers can learn from the acting profession.

> It is hard to imagine that we could survive in this world without actors. Acting serves as the quintessential social lubricant, and as a device for protecting our interests and gaining advantage in every aspect of life.
>
> Marlon Brando

If we are to believe Marlon Brando, we can gain advantage by being actors, and this is essential in public speaking because we need to gain the advantage to ensure our audience listens. Public speaking is like acting, in that you only become proficient by doing it, and role-playing public speaking is a fantastic way to improve your technique, build your confidence and get used to the sound of your own voice. This is important, as a successful public speaker or presenter is essentially selling himself, and it is difficult to sell yourself if you have poor technique, and you demonstrate your lack of confidence.

The following is adapted from an acting methodology proposed by Gottesman & Mauro (1999). I have adapted the thespian methodology into a seven-step public speaking methodology.

Step 1

Develop a warm-up routine to prepare your voice and mind for your presentation.

Step 2

Carry out a series of exercises to identify your specific strengths. In our society, we seem to value modesty, but this is misplaced when you are standing in front of an audience.

Step 3

Research and rehearsal ideas including the skill of visualisation. Putting yourself into the moment of presentation is another coaching/NLP technique.

Step 4

Plan your 'costume and props' to look and feel your professional best.

Step 5

Ah To Communicate! - Actually doing it.

Step 6
Investigate the role and aspirations of your audience.

Step 7
Put all the steps together and do a dress rehearsal. I'll then wrap up with some advice for the day of your presentation.

STEP 1

Warm-Up

All actors know that the secret to a good performance is good preparation. You will have heard that practice makes perfect. Well, I don't think that we can expect a perfect presentation, but we can maximise our potential. Unfortunately, when we are put under stress, our whole physiology reacts. This is especially lethal for someone about to do a public presentation when one of the first effects is for the throat to dry up. ARGH !!!!!!!

Don't Panic!!!!!!

Your Warm-up Routine.

Practice a warm up routine in the days leading up to your presentation. I'll show you just three exercises that will be enough to get you through any situation of public speaking.

This will only take a few minutes and the results will be worth it.

Exercise 1 - Breathing

If you are likely to become nervous, the first thing that will happen is your heart rate will rise and with it, your breathing rate. If you allow this to continue, you will hyperventilate and eventually your body will compensate by fainting. But remember you can control your breathing rate by simply being aware of it. You control your body, it does not control you. Learn to control your breathing in advance of your speaking engagement by completing this exercise regularly.

1. Sit on a straight-backed chair.

2. Feet on the floor.

3. Head up.

4. Breathe slowly in through your nose to a count of three, filling up your lungs, making your chest rise. Do not breathe from the stomach as this breathing is shallow and does not get the full volume of oxygen into the lungs.

5. Hold for a count of three.

6. Breathe out slowly through your mouth for a count of three.

7. Rest for a count of three.

8. Start at point four again.

Make this your pattern for breathing and use it before you begin speaking, because as you slow down your breathing, your brain registers that there is nothing to worry about and slows your heart rate down. This pattern of breathing may seem a little awkward at first because for most people, it is alien to think about controlling one's breathing. However, physiologically, it is the most efficient way to breathe.

Exercise 2 - Relaxing the Muscles - Banish Stress

Sit on the chair in exactly the same way as in your breathing exercise. This exercise is based on purposely tensing muscles and feeling the relief when you relax them. This will move the lactic acid out of your muscles that make them feel tense and tired. Do your breathing exercise throughout.

1. Starting with the toes, tense them up tighter and tighter to a count of 15 and relax for 5.

2. Now tense the calves, tense for 15 and release for 5.

3. Now the quads, tense for 15, release for 5.

4. Work up each muscle group to the shoulders and neck.

5. Then stand and shake it all out.

6. Now sit down and do 5 or 6 cycles of breathing.

7. Feeling Good!!!!!.

Exercise 3 - Let Your Voice 'Chill'

Nothing will show your nerves and start your own panic cycle more than a dry throat, so relax, have a drink of water and consciously let your voice 'chill' and use this phrase to get your voice ready:

BILLY BOUGHT A BAG OF BUNS AND ATE THEM IN A HURRY.
SIMON CRIED IN SAUCY SYNTAX "BILLY WHERE'S MY MONEY?"

Sound each syllable clearly and repeat three of four times.
Now simulate a yawn or do one for real.
Now repeat the sentence again out loud whilst you are in the middle of yawning.

BILLY BOUGHT A BAG OF BUNS AND ATE THEM IN A HURRY.
SIMON CRIED IN SAUCY SYNTAX "BILLY WHERE'S MY MONEY?

How did your voice change as you yawned, deeper, more resonance? Notice the range of your voice. This is because your throat was wide open. Now repeat the sentence three more times with the same feeling of the open throat. This will be pretty strange at the beginning, but persevere as you will be maximising you vocal range, but within the natural envelope for your voice. If, when you are speaking, you find you are speaking faster and faster, and the pitch of your voice is rising, pause, and replay this exercise in your head and notice how your pace and range return to normal.

Again, practice this daily leading up to your presentation.

Confidence Building

The secret about building confidence is to concentrate on the positive experiences from your past and use them as the foundation on which to build your future. Tony Robbins, in the book, 'Awake the Giant Within', calls these reference experiences. Imagine going on a journey back through your past pushing a large shopping trolley. Starting with today, what is that you have achieved today that has been a boost to your confidence. What made **you feel good**? If every day were a success building on the previous day's success, how would you feel? If you knew that you **could not fail**, what would you do differently? How would you change your approach to new challenges or opportunities?

Now push your shopping trolley back to yesterday or last week or whenever you last achieved something that built up **your confidence.** Perhaps you completed a report, passed an exam or completed a journey. Put this into your trolley. Now go further back collecting success and confidence. Think carefully, take your time, perhaps actually physically walk back along a line. Go right back as far as you can remember into childhood. Now look at the pile of success and confidence that is in your trolley. I would put money on the fact that you have more in your trolley than you would have thought. These are **your talents for success** upon which your confidence has been built. WOW, how can you fail?

Now I want you to push your full trolley back to today. Now wait just a few moments. Contemplate all that you have done in your life and now push your trolley forward to that public speaking date. Now live in that moment, with all your success and confidence.

Now before you forget, write down all those things upon which your confidence is built and keep it with you as you build up to the forthcoming speaking arrangement.

STEP 2

Interpreting Yourself, or Who are You?

We are constantly acting, bringing forward different parts of our character. However, because society has taught us that to be accepted we have to conform to a mould, we actually lose ourselves. What we need to find out is who we really are. Who we were before we were told who we should be, what we should do, before we learned that the first answer is always no. When we have identified who we are, we can then begin to understand our values, talents and skills. Try this exercise.

Exercise	Consider these simple questions and write down your answers.

Q. Who do you admire most, living or dead, historic or fictional?

Q. Why this person?

Q. What did they do?

Q. Why do they stand out?

You will end up with a set of values that you admire in someone else. However, these values are actually a reflection of your own values. This is starting to get to the heart of the authentic you.

When I first did this exercise, I chose George Thomas, Viscount Tonypandy, a previous Speaker of the House Of Commons.

Why?

He was born a few miles away from where I was born in the coalfields of the South Wales Valleys. His destiny was set in concrete the day he was born to be a minor, but he rose from obscurity to holding one of the highest positions in the country. As Mr. Speaker, he presided over the political debates that became our laws. But years before that, as Secretary of State for Wales at the time of the Abervan disaster that killed the children of an entire school, he stood up for the people against his own government, to have the coal heaps removed after the government went back on their word.

His main value was social justice for all. He strongly believed that everyone had intrinsic value, should have a voice and be able to forge their own destiny. He believed that hard work should be enough to enable anyone to become a success. He was also a humble man who never forgot his roots.

Thus, my values from this exercise were: justice, hard-work, fairness, everyone has value and never forget your roots,

What are your results? Write them here.

These traits sum up your uniqueness as an individual. Understanding your uniqueness enables you to speak from a place of authority and authenticity, thereby building rapport with your audience.

Identifying your Assets

Locked inside your head behind the fog of self-modesty, lack of confidence, self-doubt, etc, etc, your inner voice knows exactly who you are and what you believe in. This speed writing exercise is designed to let your inner voice get its way for a few minutes and to tell you what to write. To get the most out of this exercise, you must write for a full five minutes without thinking. You just write. If you run out of things to write, just write anything until your mind begins to concentrate and rescue you through life's usual noise. Take a pencil and a sheet of paper and write:

The true ME is special because.............

After a full five minutes look back over what you have written and begin to understand what you can bring to your audience out of your natural assets. Those assets that make you special, unique, that makes you worth listening to.

Now consolidate all you have learned in Step 2 into a statement of your prowess as a public speaker. Don't edit, don't be modest, just write it out and be honest.

STEP 3

Visualise a Successful Presentation

> If somebody asked me to put in one sentence what acting was, I should say that acting is the art of persuasion. The actor persuades himself first and through himself, the audience.
>
> Sir Laurence Olivier

Firstly, complete your breathing and relaxation exercise and read your summary of step 2.

One of the temptations of inexperienced individuals who have to give a presentation or 'do public speaking' is that they just copy what they have seen before. Don't do it. I cannot remember how many times I have seen someone pull out a ream of paper and say 'I have just a few notes.'

Authenticity will bring its own originality.

The exercises that you have already done should have proved your individuality. Therefore, celebrate that individuality and visualise the authentic you as a fantastically successful public speaker.

IF is a wonderful word that you can own.

Constantin Stanislavski said:

"IF acts as a lever to lift us out of the world of actuality, into the realm of possibility."

I would add to that by saying if you take on board the exercises that you complete in this volume, your world of actuality will daily be filled with new possibility. Possibility that will make you an expert public speaker.

Take five minutes to do another speed writing exercise.

Exercise

Without thinking and rationalising, take a pen and paper and write for five minutes about the success that you are going to have with your public speaking. Again don't edit, don't rationalise and don't hold back.

STEP 4

Walk the Walk

> It is always important to me, in a character part, to be able to satisfy myself with my visual appearance. I imagine at rehearsals how I hope to look, but if my makeup comes out well at the dress rehearsal, my confidence is increased a hundred fold.
>
> Sir John Gielgud

Firstly, you should do your daily breathing exercise, your relaxation exercise and your yawning exercise. With these and the voice pitch exercise, you should now be coming more used to the sound of your voice and how to manipulate it. You should also be getting used to fending off nerves with your exercises, and building your confidence.

To continue with building your confidence, you should begin to write down positive affirmations about yourself. Again, do not be self-conscious about this, but rather celebrate it, and your achievements. Complete the following sentences and then continue by writing your own.

I was complimented recently because...

....
....
....
....

....
....
....
....
....

I was particularly gratified recently when someone told me that...

....
....
....
....

I am an excellent public speaker because...

....
....
....
....

So how is your total package coming along? This concept of the total package is important because it is the entire package that your audience will be listening to and looking at. Whilst I was reporting in Kosovo, a seasoned presenter from the BBC once said to me that 80% of the impact that I would have on my audience was not what I said, but how I said it and how I looked. At first thought, this may sound incorrect because it is the content that is important. However, we now live in a highly visual, highly judgmental world. A world where someone can be a celebrity for being a size zero, or having the most outrageous wardrobe. For a spokesman, presenter, journalist or public speaker, it is essential to realise this, so that you can dress, speak and act in such a way that these things are invisible to those looking on. In other words, ensure this superficiality does not get in the way of your message.

As noted by Sir John Gielgud, your 'visual appearance and your makeup' if they work well for your presentation, will increase your confidence a hundred fold. So don't allow such simple things to detract from your message or your confidence. You have already completed an exercise on what to wear. All I would add at this stage is that you avoid small geometric patterns as these can cause annoying effects on TV screens. Also, if you are being interviewed in front of a blue screen, it is essential that you wear a contrasting colour, however, the producer of the program should advise you of such things before you arrive at the studio.

Also, in the same way that you will research your speech or presentation, rehearse what you will wear. Don't assume that your best dress or your 'wedding suit' will fit if you haven't worn them for some time.

Remembering Your Words

Reading verbatim from a prepared script should always be considered as AN option, but as a last option. This is for many reasons.

- It does not look professional unless it is an official statement that will not require comment or questions.

- It will not enable you to generate any rapport as you will not be able to 'play off' audience reaction.

- You will not know if you are taking your audience with you, as you will not be maintaining eye contact.

- Reading will not allow you to put your character into what you are saying as you will be nervous of losing your place.

- You might as well just pass out the text.

So How Do You Use a Script?

If you have learnt what you want to say, though not by rote, you can keep the script handy as a memory jogger. This will be ok as long as you don't become overly intent on the sheets of paper. However, this will allow you to watch your audience, establish rapport and establish eye contact.

Alternatives

- Place your key points onto cards and use them to prompt what you want to say.

- Project key points on to the wall that you are facing.

- Use Power Point.

- Use auto-queue if available.

- Learn what you want to say and just say it.

- Aide Memoir.

Always remember whichever method you choose, you should have a beginning, middle, and an end to your speech. Also remember:

A = Accuracy.
B = Brevity.
C = Clarity.
D = Delivery.

Before you leave for your speaking engagement, go through a checklist.

- Your Speech.
- Copy of directions to location.
- Location of parking.
- Spare change for parking the parking meter.
- Leave with plenty of time to get to the location on time.
- Spare make-up for the ladies, comb for the gents.
- Emergency phone number of location and organiser of event.
- Mobile phone.
- Business cards.
- Sense of humour.

Organise all the above in plenty of time so that you don't have to get stressed at the last minute.

STEP 5.

AH! TO COMMUNICATE!

Firstly, repeat the following exercises:

Breathing Exercise.
Relaxation.
Yawn exercise.

If you have prepared and are quietly confident, you can then 'own the stage.' It is at this point that you will begin to understand the thrill of connection and communication. As you feel the thrill of 'just being in the moment,' you should attempt to begin embedding the feeling deep in your constitution. By exploring, embedding and amplifying this feeling, you begin to do what a coach would call 'anchoring.' Anchoring is a tool used in Neural Linguistic Programming as a reference method to 'rewire' your brain. So that next time you have to do public speaking, you will be able to recall this reference and start from a place of greater confidence than your previous speaking engagement. Thus, every experience reinforces in a positive way the previous experience, enabling you to positively look for and enjoy the next speaking engagement. Indeed, as you begin to master this methodology, you can enjoy your next speaking engagement even before you present it.

You will also find that you very soon begin to exude that almost spiritual quality of charisma that so many strive to achieve. You now know how to grow this charisma into your speaking, but keep it to yourself. It's our secret'. It is at this point that you will really be able to put the stamp of your personality into your speaking. When you know you are at your best and 'on a roll,' you will begin to really enjoy the whole experience of public speaking, as I do.

EXERCISE

You have now learnt enough for a recorded exercise. For this, you will need either a voice recorder or a video recorder. Prepare a 10 or 15-minute talk either on a subject of your own choice, or using the title 'How to give a Ten Minute Talk' using all that you have learnt so far on the subject. Then do the following:

1. Play your presentation talk back and just listen to yourself. Take no notes. Just listen to the quality of your voice, its inflection, pace etc. If you have a video recording, also look at your mannerisms, movement, use of hands etc.

2. Sit down with someone who you trust, and watch or listen to your performance together.

3. Honestly appraise your performance in terms of what you can improve upon. DO NOT MAJOR ON WHAT WENT WRONG. This serves no good aim, other than to destroy the confidence that you have been working on.

4. Make a note of where you can improve on the following:

Eye Contact	Rapport	Structure
Pace	Inflection	Interest
Movement	Humour	Accuracy
Clarity	Delivery	Breathing
Authority	Charisma	Personality
Enthusiasm	Engagement	Projection
Sincerity	Direct	Patronising

Once you and your buddy have gone through each of these points, you will have learnt an awful lot about yourself, and also how you are perceived. However, and I cannot state this strongly enough, you must make this a positive learning experience so that it is part of a building process upon which you can build a positive and growing public speaking future.

Now listen to the recording for a third time by yourself. This will be the last reflection on this speech so make the most of the exercise. Ask these questions and write down your answers.

Q. Which part of the tape are you most proud of?

....

....

....

....

....

Q. Which part of the tape seems the most important?

....

....

....

....

....

....

....

....

....

Q. Do you think the audience would have learnt anything?

....

Q. Would they have learnt what you wanted them to learn?

....

Q. What could you have done better?

....

Q. Did you observe ABCD?

....

Q. Was there a beginning, middle and end?

....

Now congratulate yourself for completing a complex, but life-enabling exercise.

STEP 6.

Your Reason d'Etre

Investigate the role and aspirations of your audience.

How are your exercises going? Don't forget the more you practice, the more competent and confident you will become.

Breathing.
Relaxation.
Yawning.

This is one of the most important and one of the simplest steps to get right. Your audience is the reason that you exist as a public speaker. We have already discussed the need for rapport, that connection that makes your transmission and their reception of information the closed loop that will bring success.

It is vital, therefore, that you pay your audience due respect by doing your homework to understand your audience and their aspirations. Some or all of the following topics will relate to your presentation.

Understand the demographic of your group by researching the following:

- Age range.

- Background.
- Specialisation.
- What are they expecting?
- What do they need to know?
- What will they take away from your presentation?
- Will they want to hear more?
- What are their aspirations?

Knowing the above will enable you to accurately target your presentation to their needs, not just your needs. After all, your object is to fulfil their needs to be 'educated', not your need to hear your own voice. If you are attentive to your audience's needs, they will not only receive what you say, but also you will see and feel their encouragement, which will spur you on, thus building your self-esteem and confidence.

Importantly, you should review this exercise every time you are going to speak, as every audience is different. An actor, for example, who has played Macbeth many times, will have a different chemistry with a new Lady Macbeth. Thus as you act the part of the public speaker, your partner, i.e. your audience, will change, and thus you must think about how you will change not only the content, but where you pitch the talk, etc.

Listening is a skill too!

Allow your audience the time to listen. This means that you deliver using a regulated, even pace with pauses, giving your audience the time to let your words sink in. If you are facilitating listening, then your audience will get much more from your presentation. This will be the difference between communication and just talking.

Maintain Control

Your audience will expect you, as the person in authority standing in front of them to maintain control. Therefore, be conscious that it is your responsibility to be constantly aware of what is happening in your presentation. Simple things like is the room to warm, is there a lack of oxygen? If people are fighting to stay awake, it may not be because your talk is sending them to sleep. If you are in a closed in room, with no flow of oxygen, no open window or air-conditioning, have a window opened or turn down the temperature. Likewise, if it's too cold, close a window or turn up the heating.

React to your audience to maintain rapport, pay attention to their mood and demeanour. You will soon see if you are losing your audience. It is here that you must react to bring them back under your control and regain their interest. This will mean you may have to change how you are speaking, or even the direction of what you are saying. Perhaps you are speaking at the wrong level, too slow, too fast. Did you make some wrong assumptions? There are many things you can do mid-presentation to keep them interested, as you would naturally in a one-to-one conversation. Be aware of this and do not 'press on regardless'; your flexibility will be essential to their understanding and interest.

STEP 7

Putting It All Together.

Firstly, do your exercises:

Breathing.
Relaxation.
Yawning.

Now re-read all your notes and answers to the completed exercises. You should see that you have completed a major journey and you will be surprised at how much you have learnt. You are ready for your first or next speaking engagement, and your confidence is rightly high. So what are you going to do now?

- Enjoy your success now.
- Prepare your talk.
- Research its content.
- Research your audience.
- Arrive early.
- Make sure the room is right.
- Give your talk.
- React to your audience's needs.
- Bathe in the admiration of your audience.

Sounds easy, doesn't it? And it is easy when you have taken into account all that you have learnt. The last thing to do, is to carry out a self-debriefing once you have completed your talk. It is important to do this so that you can continually and incrementally improve for your next talk. Complacency in your own debriefing is a lost opportunity to improve. Depending on your audience, you can also involve them in your debriefing process. You can ask for your audience to fill out debrief forms, but also hanging around for ten minutes after your talk will usually be enough for you to get feedback. Again, remember to write it down and remember to refer to it in your preparation for your next talk.

PART TWO

Specialist Crisis Presentations

Presentations in a time of crisis need specific and sensitive handling. When panic is ensuing and complex situations are unfolding, the spokesperson, whether trained or untrained, planned or unplanned, will become the face of the situation to the media or to the organisation. These situations could be anything from a plummeting share price or market share, a fire that destroys a business, or a terrorist attack. The person briefing may be the organisation's Public Relations Officer (PRO), or equally it could be you if you are the only one available. As I stated before, the ABCD will get you through 'first contact', but you may need a more formal presentation as a follow up. Most large organisations will have a PRO who will have pre-empted many situations that you are likely to experience. One of the roles of the PRO will be to produce a book of questions called something like 'Press Lines' or 'Media Messages'. These should be readily available to give enough information to answer most questions. The PRO will have committed them to memory, but if you are the only one available, irrespective of the media clamour for answers, take a few minutes to see if what you need to brief is already in the book, it will save you effort and anxiety. If your organisation does not have a book of press lines, have one written now. It can be a straightforward exercise for smaller organisations, but specialist help is sometimes required for large organisations, from companies such as www.know-no-bounds.com. If you do not have prepared press lines then brainstorm potential issues. Imagine the questions that the press, or your boss could ask, and then provide the written answers for you future reference.

Providing Presentation Answers Using Message Mapping.

The message map is a tool for anyone having to brief in a crisis situation, or as a tool to construct complex presentations. The message map was presented to the World Health Organisation in October 2002 by Vincent T Covello PhD, and has been adopted by many government and private organisations. You will see that it is an evolution of the lotus method described earlier in this book.

Message Map Template

Key Message 1	Key Message 2
Supporting Fact 1.1	Supporting Fact 2.1
Supporting Fact 1.2	Supporting Fact 2.2
Supporting Fact 1.3	Supporting Fact 2.3

Covello states that the message map achieves eight important risk communication goals:

1. Identifying stakeholders early in the communication process.

2. Anticipating stakeholder questions and concerns BEFORE they are raised.

3. Organising thinking and developing prepared messages in response to anticipated stakeholder questions and concerns.

4. Developing key messages and supporting information within a clear, concise, transparent and accessible framework.

5. Promoting open dialogue about messages both inside and outside the organisation.

6. Providing user-friendly guidance to spokespersons and journalists.

7. Ensuring that the organisation has a central repository of consistent messages.

8. Encouraging the organisation to speak with one voice.

In generating the message, the process can be as important as the end message. The first step would be to get all the stakeholders together, and here is your first obstacle. For as soon as you get, say, six stakeholders together with a vested interest in the outcome, you will get at least seven opinions. But it is also here that the message mapping can come into its own by prioritising and removing emotion from the process. Also of note is where your message map shows up gaps. In these areas, you need to do a gap analysis with your stakeholders, as this will show where your message will have gaps also.

The Seven Steps.

There are seven steps to the construction of a message map.

Step 1.

The first step is to identify the stakeholders. These are the individuals who have influence, interest, or are affected by the preparation and delivery of the presentation or media brief. It is important to think carefully to ensure that all stakeholders are involved.

<u>Stakeholders could include</u>

- Victims.
- Victim families.
- Directly affected individuals.
- Emergency response professionals.
- Public health personnel.
- Law enforcement personnel.
- Hospital personnel.
- Government agencies.
- Politicians.
- Unions.
- The media – all types.
- Legal professionals
- Contractors.

- Consultants.
- Suppliers/Vendors.
- Local residents.
- Minority groups.
- Special needs groups.
- Advisory panels.
- The Business community.
- Local religious leaders.

Step 2.

The second step is to identify the specific concerns of the stakeholders. Specific concerns are generated through research, though you could also use a mind map to generate concerns. Areas you should research include:

- Media – especially as this is now seeking news 24/7.
- Web sites.
- Document review including 'Press lines'.
- Review of complaint logs, telephone logs and media history.
- Interviews with subject matter experts.
- Facilitated discussion sessions.
- Focus groups.
- Surveys.

Research has shown that up to 95% of stakeholder concerns will be raised when steps one and two are followed through in a thorough systematic analysis of stakeholder information.

Step 3.

The third step in message map construction is to analyse the specific concerns to identify common trends and general concerns. Research has shown that most high-level concerns are associated with no more than 15-25 primary underlying concerns. General concerns could include:

- Immediate actions.
- Making the area secure.
- Making the area safe.
- Recording and collection of evidence.
- Health and safety concerns.
- Environmental concerns.
- Quality of life.
- Equity/fairness.
- Cultural impact.
- Legal and regulatory.
- Basic information. Who, What, When, Where, Why, How?
- Openness and disclosure.
- Accountability.
- Options and alternatives.
- Control
- Effects on community.
- Long-term health implications.
- Will it unbalance the status quo?
- Listening/caring/empathy.
- Relationship building.

Step 4.

The forth step in message mapping is to develop key messages in response to stakeholder concerns, both general and specific. Brainstorming and mind mapping sessions can be used to produce message narratives, usually in the form of complete sentences that are entered as key messages onto the message map. Alternately, the brainstorming can produce keywords for each method, which are again entered into the message map. Keywords will act as an aide memoir or the bones of your presentation on which to place the flesh, i.e. the detail, later on.

Key Messages are based on the most important issues for your target audience, these will include:

- What they most **need** to know.
- What they most **want** to know.
- What they are most **concerned** about.

It is essential to remember that especially in crisis situations, reasonable people act unreasonably. Journalists especially are more interested in column inches than you presenting cold facts and they may try to bully you into a story. I have seen it and experienced it. Don't fall for it. Also, when you are placed under pressure, stick to your key messages. Burn them into your brain, otherwise the pressure can get to you. In those situations, you could either dry up or get stuck in auto-rant. Don't let it happen. Be aware of it and deal with it.

Crisis Briefing

So you now have key messages that portray your message.

ACCURATELY - A.

They should be three or four words long and when spoken less than nine seconds in duration, or 27 seconds for a set of three key messages.

BRIEFLY – B.

The messages should be brief but completely understandable by a thirteen-year-old.

CLEARLY – C.

Only one meaning should be possible, and that must be the meaning that you as presenter intended.

DO YOU RECOGNISE A PATTERN?

Step 5.

Next, you need to develop the underlying facts to support your key messages. The methods that you used to write your key messages should be used to develop the supporting facts. Again, you should adopt the ABC methodology.

Step 6.

The next step is to test your messages and supporting statements on an audience, perhaps just two or three people who are subject experts, but who have not been involved in producing your message map. The test that you are looking for is that they receive all the facts of the incidents and that you can answer all their questions from your supporting statements. If this is not the case, go back to the team that constructed the message map with you and 'test and adjust' until all the issues are covered.

Step 7.

The last step is to deliver the brief or presentation. If you are confident, you can do this directly from the message map. If you need some extra support, you can write your brief out in full. You can also use your message map to construct a press release. When presenting from your message map, you should follow these guidelines.

- Pick one of your key messages as a deliberate sound bite. Open your presentation with it and reinforce the presentation by repeating it at the end.

- Make sure you keep the sound bite to its planned nine-second length. If you elaborate or change it in your presentation, the audience or media may miss it.

- If you are asked a question, use the words from your message map. Give them your key point, reinforce your key point and summarise using what you have already told them.

- Stay on message and don't waffle.

- Take advantage of any questions to re-emphasise your key message or use the question to bridge to another key point.

- Keep messages short and focused.

- Always be totally honest and retain your integrity at all costs.

- You do not have to answer every question there and then.

- It is your agenda so pass on the planned information.

- You are not there just to provide copy for journalists, so don't give in to pressure.

- It is perfectly fine to take a question to answer at a later press conference or to set up a separate interview.

So what does a completed message map look like? Here is one developed from an incident in Kosovo:

REDUCING WEAPONS HANDLING FATALITIES

Key Message 1	Key Message 2
Weapons Kill.	Weapons-handling is for military personnel only
Supporting Fact 1.1	Supporting Fact 2.1
Twenty-four child deaths in the past twelve months.	Civilians have not been trained on how to make weapons and munitions safe.
Supporting Fact 1.2	Supporting Fact 2.2
Each death was completely avoidable.	Many of the munitions are now unstable as they have been exposed to the elements for almost three years.

Try this method to develop a crisis brief or any other brief; it is simple, straightforward, and will guide you through the most complex situations to a consolidated and intelligent brief.

In Conclusion

In working through this handbook, you will now know the essence of what I have learned about practical public speaking. What I cannot teach is the actual confidence that comes from doing public speaking. That confidence will only come from you doing all you can to prepare for your speaking engagement and then actually getting in front of groups of people and enjoying the experience. After thoroughly completing all the exercises, including doing your presentations in front of the mirror, you will be ready for any presentation in any environment.

Enjoy the buzz, it will be fun and you will learn so much about your subject and yourself.

BECAUSE NOW

YES YOU CAN DO PUBLIC SPEAKING!!!!

Additional notes and resource

Quotable Quotes

An excellent way to start any talk.

Action springs not from thought, but from a readiness for responsibility.

Dietrich Bonhoffer.

Put it before them briefly so they will read it, clearly so that they will appreciate it, picturesquely so they will remember it and above all, accurately so they will be guided by its light.

Joseph Pulitzer.

The art of being wise is the art of knowing what to overlook.

William James.

The finest eloquence is that which gets things done.

David Lloyd George.

Success is the ability to go from one failure to another with no loss of enthusiasm.

Winston Churchill.

Opportunity dances with those who are already on the dance floor.

H. Jackson Brown Jr.

If at first you don't succeed, you are running above average.

M.H Alderson.

Great works are performed not by strength, but by perseverance.

Samuel Johnson

Plan your routine, routinely plan.

Tony Kenneson-Adams.

The notes I handle no better than many other pianists. But the pauses between the notes – ah, that is where the art resides.

Arthur Schnabel.

I was playing all the right notes, but not necessarily in the right order.

Eric Morecombe.

Does anyone have any questions for my answers.

Henry Kissinger.

The secret of your future is hidden in your daily routine.

Mike Murdock.

We cannot become what we need to be, remaining what we are.

Max Depree

Action may not always bring happiness; but there is no happiness without action.

Benjamin Disraeli.

Some cause happiness wherever they go, others whenever they go.

Oscar Wilde.

The ultimate measure of a man is not where he stands in moments of comfort, but where he stand in moments of challenge and controversy.

Martin Luthur King Jr.

It's what you learn after you know it all that counts.

John Wooden.

To the man who only has a hammer in his tool kit, every problem is a nail.

Abraham Maslow.

Not everything that can be counted counts, and not everything that counts can be counted.

Albert Einstein.

The best way to have a good idea is to have lots of ideas.

Linus Pauling.

The trouble with the world is that the stupid are cocksure and the intelligent are full of doubt.

Bertrand Russell.

The indispensable first step to getting the things you want out of life is this: decide what you want.

Ben Stein.

Of all the liars in the world, sometimes the worst are your own fears.

Rudyard Kipling

The fearless are merely fearless. People who act in spite of their fears are truly brave.

James A, LaFond-Lewis.

Sour, sweet, bitter, pungent, all must be tasted.

Chinese Proverb.

Happy people plan actions, they don't plan results.

Dennis Waitely.

Eighty percent of life is just showing up.

Woody Allen.

If in the last few years, you haven't discarded a major opinion or acquired a new one, check your pulse. You may be dead.

Gelett Burgess..

The best defence is a strong offence, and I intend to start offending right now.

Captain James T Kirk.

BIBLIOGRAPHY

Covello, V. T. (2002) *Message Mapping, Risk Communication, and Bio-terrorism.* Paper Presented at the World Health Organisation Workshop on Bio-terrorism and Risk Communication Geneva, Switzerland, October 1, 2002.

Enright, D. (2001) *The Wicked Wit of Winston Churchill.* London: Michael O'Mara Books Ltd.

Gottesman, D., & Mauro, B. (1999) *The Interview Rehearsal Book.* New York: Berkley Publishing Group.

Kushner, M., & Yeung, R. (2007) *Public Speaking for Dummies.* Chichester, England: John Wiley & Sons, Ltd.

Zweibel, B. *GottaGettaBlog.* www.ggci.com, accessed 8 Jan 2007

WHAT IS NLP (NEURO LINGUSTIC PROGRAMMING?

Neuro Linguistic Programming was created and developed in the early 70s by Richard Bandler and John Grinder via their studies at the University of California at Santa Cruz. This was no ordinary study, their use of technology from linguistics and information science, combined with insights from behavioural psychology and general systems theory were used to unlock the secrets and magic of highly effective communication.

The creators of NLP were interested in how people influence one another, and in the possibility of being able to duplicate the behaviours and therefore performance of highly effective and influential people.

The methodology and specific NLP technology makes it possible to discover much of what the human brain does that he or she is not aware of.

The word **Neuro** refers to an understanding of the brain and its functioning. **Linguistic** relates to the human communication aspects (verbal and non verbal) and **programming** is the behavioural and thinking patterns processed by the human brain.

For more information on NLP, I recommend:

Neuro Linguistic programming for dummies
Romilla Ready & Kate Burton
ISBN 9 780764 570285

Yes! You Can Start Your Own Business

By David Knight
CEO
The Executive Solution

"Nine out of ten new businesses fail within the first five years"
Robert T Kiyosaki Author of *Rich Dad Poor Dad*

DON'T BE ANOTHER STATISTIC

Do you want to start your own Business?

If so then YES! YOU CAN START YOUR OWN BUSINESS is the perfect solution for you!

David Knight takes the reader through a no holds barred guide through the process of starting up your own business.

Knight's unique award winning guide is written in a way which feels like the reader embarks on their business journey with a friend guiding them through each step in a down to earth fun filled read of a book

Visit

www.TheExecutiveSolution.co.uk

Look out for

YES! YOU CAN GET THAT JOB

YES! YOU START YOUR OWN CHILDCARE BUSINESS

YES! YOU CAN START YOUR OWN COACHING BUSINESS

YES! YOU CAN MEASURE THE BENEFITS OF COACHING

Coming summer 2007

More great titles from The Executive Solution

English edition 2007

The Executive Solution Ltd publishing division are passionate about working with only the best authors and leaders within the world of Business.

If you feel that you have exceptional talent and would like to be considered for a future project then please contact us at feedback@theexecutivesolution.co.uk

This book is also available as a limited edition audio CD

More information below

www.TheExecutiveSolution.co.uk

www.ingramcontent.com/pod-product-compliance
Ingram Content Group UK Ltd.
Pitfield, Milton Keynes, MK11 3LW, UK
UKHW020200200726
13856UKWH00003B/1099